Gain Self-Confidence Fast With NLP

Effective N...   ...niques
That Will ...   ...eem
Radically Fo... ... Life - Positive
Psychol... ...oaching Series

By Ian Tuhovsky

Copyright © 2014

All rights reserved. No part of this publication may be reproduced, stored in a retrieval system, or transmitted, in any form or by any means, electronic, mechanical, photocopying, recording or otherwise without the prior written permission of the author and the publishers.

Table of Contents:

Chapter 1 What is NLP?   9
Chapter 2 NLP Techniques   12
Chapter 3 NLP During Your Self-Confidence Boost Journey   28
Chapter 4 NLP to Maintain High Self-Confidence Forever and Never Feel Insecure Again   37
Conclusion – Your Personal Success for Life   51
Recommended Reading for You: 55

<u>My Mailing list</u>: If you would like to receive fresh info about **new Kindle reads** on social dynamics, psychology, career, NLP, success and healthy living for **free** (or deeply **discounted – as low as $0,99**) <u>I invite you to my Mailing List.</u> Whenever my new book is out, I set the promotional price/free period for two days. You will get an e-mail notification and will **be the first to get the book for $0,99 (or free)** during its limited promotion.

Why would I do this when it took me countless hours to write these e-books?

First of all, that's my way of saying **"thank you"** to my new readers. Second of all – **I want to spread the word about my books and ideas.** Mind you that **I hate spam and e-mails that come too frequently** - no worries about that.
If you think that's a good idea and are in, just surf there: http://eepurl.com/R_UhP

Please be aware that every book and "short read" I publish is written truly by me, with thoroughly researched content 100% of the time. Unfortunately, **there's a huge number of low quality, cheaply outsourced spam titles on Kindle**

3

non-fiction market these days, created by various Internet marketing companies. I don't tolerate these books. I want to provide you with high quality, so if you think that one of my books/short reads can be improved anyhow, please contact me at coachingpositivepsychology@gmail.com.

I will be very happy to hear from you, because that's who I write my books for.

<u>Introduction</u> Why NLP For Self-Esteem?

I want to thank you and congratulate you for buying the book "Gain Self-Confidence Fast with NLP". I wrote it to share my personal experience with NLP so as to encourage you to transform yourself your very own way. If I could do it - you can do it too. The truth is that very often we are the slaves of our own mind. There are way too many limitations imposed upon us by the society we are born in. There are also cultural 'traditions' or 'ways to do things right'. Hopefully, you enjoy this read and make your own decision- it's your life. So keep creating it and improving it with NLP! Let's restore happiness, passion and freedom!

Even though I was young, I will never forget the memory: my family was at the city public pool, and I was four years old. I had always been a 'water baby' and knew how to swim before I could even walk. My uncle, a man who strangely made almost two hundred jumps skydiving but was still afraid of heights if he could see the ground, looked at the really high-diving board, the one that looked like it had risen into the sky like a skyscraper, where all the "real" divers would practice all their fancy dives, and said "I could never jump off that thing!". I looked at this looming tower of a high-diving board and remember thinking, "Hmmmm....I could do that!" I climbed up the ladder, got to the edge, and looked down—oh boy, that's when the fear hit! I turned around to climb back down the ladder but there were already other people just waiting on the ladder for their turn. I could not get back down, so I went to the edge of the diving board again, looked at the deep, bright blue, far-away water, closed my eyes, held my arms out at my sides, and jumped! By the end of the day, I had jumped off that diving board so many times that the undersides of my arms were red from hitting the water at such a fast velocity. I had a blast! (Of course, as an adult, in retrospect, I look back and wonder, "What in the world was the city lifeguard thinking letting a four-year old jump off that high of a diving board?!")

Contrastingly, I remember the first time in my adult life when I truly understood what other people meant when they would say the proverbial "it just hit me like a ton of bricks." I was watching a repeat of a popular television show, an episode I had actually seen several times before, but for some unknown reason, THIS time I heard the main character ask a question that I had never paid attention to in the past, and it took my breath away: "When did life stop being fun, and start being scary?"

It was an "aha!" moment in life! Things did used to be fun! And life did feel scary as an adult! I tried to recall what life felt like when it was just plain fun, where the words "confidence" and "self-esteem" did not exist in my brain, because they **were already a part of who I was!** Like playing on the covered porch outside in the freezing cold just because I liked to hear, see, and smell the rain, or when I would line up in kindergarten for a turn at the 'big kid' swings just because they could swing higher and I could fly faster. Do you remember how as kids we would wait until that crucial, perfectly-timed moment of "Now!" so we could leap off the swing at its highest peak, fly through the air, and land in the sand? Even though there was some kind of natural fear, like when I had been looking off that diving board, LIFE was not scary. Where had that confidence gone, and, frankly, when did it leave?

So what is the answer? How does a person make life fun again? How do we re-gain that inherent self-confidence and self-esteem which we were born with so that we can make our lives more fulfilling, successful and, dare I say it, even happy?

The answer is in using one of the simplest, easiest, most fundamental tools that we as humans have at our disposal: a scientific practice called Neuro-Linguistic Programming, or

NLP. NLP is a set of tools and techniques that will give you back the power to change your thought processes, and in turn, re-direct the course of your life. It is vital to boosting your willpower, changing your mindset, and is the true key to gaining the natural and permanent self-confidence that you so strongly desire. If you choose to harness this power, to utilize these techniques, I guarantee you will come to see how you can swiftly 'change your fate,' so to speak, and become more confident to a degree you never thought possible.

So welcome, friends! Congratulations on choosing this book to help you begin your journey of radiant empowerment, confidence, and self-esteem! Let the adventure begin!

Chapter 1 What is NLP?

Neuro-Linguistic Programming, although it sounds intimidating and uber-scientific, is simply a fancy name for something that you actually already know: broken down, "Neuro" is neurologically how your brain works; "Linguistic" is language; and "Programming" is simply a pattern of behavior you learn through experience. Translated, it simply means that you will be using your actions to change the way your brain processes your language, and in turn your language will reflect the new way that your brain is thinking. So in essence, NLP functions in a circle; it is about directing the chain of events, thoughts, reactions, behaviors, and emotions in life, and using simple techniques to re-train your brain to become who and what you want to be. In the NLP cycle, how you think influences how you feel, which in turn influences how you react to situations.

Regarding our neurological systems, our view of the world is formed by the information we collect using all of our physical and emotional senses and intuitions.

When you learn the techniques of NLP, you will no longer be lost in a fog of emotion, unable to clearly see what is around you due to your convoluted emotional responses. Feelings and emotions fluctuate. Solid foundations of choices of thoughts and behaviors are the firm basis to regulate the sometimes-rollercoaster of your inconsistent emotions. You will see clearly, and will be mindful of your own thoughts in order to bring about the outcomes you desire.

As with any tool, it can be seen as a gift or a curse. Both self-empowering and self-defeating thoughts have ways of manifesting themselves into your life's reality. Certainly, as anyone understands, sometimes 'life just happens.' There will always be outside forces that happen to us that are outside of our control. The fundamental key of NLP is not to channel positive energy from external forces to affect the direction of our lives; it is how we can learn to imbed the tools inside of ourselves in order to control our actions and, subsequently, our reactions.

This is the beauty of Neuro-Linguistic Programming: it gives you the tools and techniques to change how you THINK, so that you are able to change how you FEEL, so that you can change how you REACT, and henceforth alter the outcomes in your life. This tool forms the true necessary foundation upon which to build your life; although it can be used negatively, you have chosen this book because you want to make a POSITIVE difference. NLP presents techniques that are used to change our habits, our will, and even can alter our personalities. Habits are not confined simply to our external actions; humans have just as many emotional customs as they have physical routines, and these behaviors affect the paths of our lives.

I am reminded of a story I heard a long time ago: a man is sitting on his front porch, rocking comfortably in his porch swing, talking pleasantly with his neighbor. Then they hear the telephone ring inside the house. The neighbor looks at the man and asks, "Aren't you going to go answer that?" The man wisely replies, "I own my phone. My phone does not own me."

I think often we as a society, even as a general humanity, forget the wisdom in that story: we as people own our emotions, our thoughts, our actions, our choices—they do not own us. WE are in control. We are not victims—we are the masters of ourselves, to face the joys and sorrows that life hands us with personal ownership, and not a sense of martyrdom. So how do we begin to harness this sense of personal empowerment and ownership over ourselves?

Chapter 2 NLP Techniques

My favorite example of defining a daily goal is a piece of advice a friend gave me. This friend was a career-military cargo pilot, and at one time he underwent advanced survival training for the wilderness in case of being stranded in emergency circumstances. He was taught that above all, there is one thing to focus on, and one thing only: work every moment of every day to do something to improve your situation. For him that meant perhaps finding shelter or a source of water or a source of food off the land, or even simply creating a fire—he did everything he could in every circumstance to improve his situation. This is a wonderfully wise overall goal to apply to your everyday life: work EVERY DAY to improve your situation, no matter how big or small.

If you have never had a high level of self-confidence or high self-esteem, you may not realize that it will have a dramatic impact on all areas of your life. Even just committing yourself to a process of change will affect your life and even add to your self-confidence and self-esteem.

Here are ten ways that these new found things will impact your life:

•   You will ultimately be more resistant to inevitable complications in life. This is due to the fact that you will be far less likely to admit defeat or surrender to hopelessness.

•   You will be more self-confident in what you can achieve, so that you will be more willing to be imaginative, inventive and original. All of these qualities lead to higher rates of success, both personally and professionally, and more achievement and tangible results. Have you ever wondered how many geniuses and prodigies this world never knew just because they never had courage to show off?

•   You will be more aspiring in every aspect of your life because you will have confidence in the fact that you can realize your objectives.

•   You will have more encouraging and caring connections with others. When you have high self-esteem you tend to gravitate toward people who have the same. Those who are self-confident tend to attract the same type of people. Quality attracts quality.

- You will show respect through your actions by showing others much respect, adoration, and care. You will no longer see them as a danger or a threat to you. You will find that others will treat you the same in return.

- You will be more optimistic in general. You will anticipate that good things will happen.

- You will experience greatly decreased anxiety because you will become secure with your capability to cope with difficulty. You will be able to put that formerly-negative brain power into something productive and beneficial for yourself instead.

- You will be more of a risk-taker. It is a proven fact that successful people are prepared to take chances. Certainly there is the fear of failure, and certainly many people do fail. However, sometimes you just know deep within yourself that you should pursue something, come hell or high water; these tools will give you the confidence to pursue your dreams and seek out your adventures.

- You will be a much more social person. You will no longer be reluctant to meet new people or engage strangers. Every time you meet someone new it could be a new pal, business associate, client, date or maybe even your second half!

- You will be able to take criticism and use it to further develop yourself. You will be so confident that when someone says something critical it will not hurt, but will instead be helpful for self-evaluation and growth. You will be able to gauge if it is something you can use to better yourself.

Notice the frequent usage of the phrase "you will." The word "will" is not tentative or weak, such as "could"; the word "will" is a word of faith, of determination, of even demanding that life gives you more than you have received. So believe in the "will" of these ten points, not the "could" or the "should"—you WILL be a more confident person!

In German, "will" means "I want to" (the full phrase is: "Ich will"- "I want to"). English and German have the same Germanic roots. Many words are interconnected. The linguistics experts point the fact that the English word "will" come from the German word "wollen "("to want") and the Latin word "velle "- "wish ". In English, the word "will " is mainly used to indicate the future tense or to express the inevitable events.

So...why don't you make your personal success something inevitable?

NLP has many techniques and tools that you can use to increase your levels of self-confidence and self-esteem. Here are a few that helped me in insurmountable ways to boost myself confidence levels. Even at my level of expertise, it is important to continually remember the basics, so I still utilize these every single day.

ANCHORING

Anchoring is the act of tying a feeling and an action/phrase/etc. (anchors) together in the brain. It is technically called neuro-associative conditioning.

You attach the great feeling that you want to f(
to a trigger. It may be a movement, a phras
anything you would like. When you use that trigg
bring on the same feeling all over again.

1. Choose a unique trigger. Make sure it is not something you say or do all the time. I squeeze my knee. You can make it whatever you like. Just make sure that it is pretty unique. You can even say a phrase in your head as an anchor, but at the beginning I'd recommend that you do it physically.

2. Pick an experience where you felt tremendous self-confident and had high self-esteem. Put yourself in that memory. Go back and be present in that moment: What do you see? What do you hear? How do you feel? What do you smell? If possible, even try to recall what you are wearing and what others around you are doing. Are you walking up the park smiling and holding hands with date of your dreams? Just got your promotion? Finally did something you've always wanted to do? It's your call. Do your best here.

3. Now focus in on how you felt being self-confident. Feel it to the fullest. Revel in it. Grow past the specifics of the memory and absorb the sensation of confidence you were experiencing.

4. When you are at the height of feeling amazing, use your trigger. You are connecting it to the feeling, to create your own patters and to reprogram your neuropsychology to associate you trigger with the experience.

5. Do this several times, using the trigger at the climax of your self-confident moment.

6. Now try using your trigger while doing normal, everyday things. If you have anchored correctly, you should immediately feel self-confident. If not, repeat steps 2-5 over and over.

Remember: The stronger emotions you are feeling during the process, the more effective anchoring will be.

SWISH

This is one of my favorite NLP tools. It works very how to practice "SWISH", doing the steps in order

1. Start in the now. Picture yourself in the situation you want to change: having low self-esteem. Pretend like you are looking at a screen with this situation playing out. Pick one of the lowest points. What is going on around you? What are you doing? What do you hear and see or even smell and taste? Feel all the emotions that you felt in that situation as you are watching it play out. Make the picture real.

2. Now you are going to picture yourself as a self-confident person with high self-esteem. Picture what you will be doing, wearing, seeing, feeling, in this situation. Make it a perfect, beautiful, happy, wonderful scene. Feel strong, confident, joyous, and content. Make it enticing and alluring to be the new you.

3. Next, you will take the scene of you in your worst state and make it big and colorful. Really experience how terrible you feel. In the middle of the scene, tiny and dark is the scene of the way you want to feel. Make it as tiny as possible as if it is pulling away from you until it is a tiny dot. Pull it back like you would a rubber band. You can feel the band get tighter and tighter.

4. Suddenly say "swooooooooooosh" while you release it and let it jump forward. It suddenly is in full view, big and bright. Look at it, watch it. Feel how much different you feel in the new you. Take it all in.

5. Now close both scenes entirely and focus on something else for a bit.

6. Repeat steps 1-4 five to ten times. Each time swooshing/swishing faster and faster. Eventually changing the scene from the current you to the new you should take less than a second.

7. Try looking at the starting scene that you want to change. If it is not automatically replaced by the scene of the confident you, start the process over again a few times.

Another important thing to remember is to stay in the now. Do not focus on what has happened or may happen. The past and future will only drain you; you cannot do anything about either one. Your power comes from the moment happening right now. This time, right now, is when you can change, be successful and make choices. Use present moment awareness to help you remember this. It will also (which is extremely powerful!) affect your prefrontal cortex – the part of your brain responsible for taking action (execution), focusing, social intelligence and control, achieving goals and many other factors. Just do it EVERY DAY and you will see what happens.

PRESENT MOMENT AWARENESS

1. Pick the same time of day every day to do this. Pick the same peaceful place to do it in as well. Make sure no one will interrupt you. Turn your phone off. Go offline. A silent room without any electronic devices inside it should be perfect (OK, you can keep your Kindle, but put it away, please).

2. You need to have a clear and calm mind. Relax your mind and body. You can stretch a little and take few deep breaths before you start. Your mind should become empty and emotionless. You may need to practice a bit in order to be able to reach such a state, if you're not used to silence and nothingness it can be a little difficult at the beginning. Make sure you are upright as you do not want to fall asleep. I do it just sitting comfortably in my favorite chair with my back straight, looking at my piano or a blank wall during the day. Some people do it looking at candle's flame in the dark. It's your call.

3. You want to stop thinking. You want to be able to come in full contact with reality as it is in that very moment. Thinking is a distraction. Repeat several times to yourself that you need to be fully aware of what is going on right in this moment and that you are releasing the past and future.

4. Keep your mind busy to keep it from thinking, but don't get too paranoid about thinking that you shouldn't be thinking. It will come with time- as you become

better at meditating you will not have to do this so much. Turn the focus of your mind to:

- Listening

Hear everything going on around you. As you are able to focus better, tune into softer sounds in the distance. Release the sounds you have just heard and focus on the present sounds.

- Feeling

Feel what your legs and arms are touching, how they are laying. Experience the feel of the clothes on your body. Feel the weight of your feet placed flat on the floor underneath. Be aware of the temperatures in your environment, how your body feels sitting in a chair, or standing in your current pose. Pay attention to any physical pain or discomfort. Feel negative feelings like anxiety. Pay attention to how all these feelings change as you meditate. Release from your mind what you just felt and focus on what you are presently feeling.

- Thinking

Pay attention to the thoughts coming and going without delving into them. Label important feelings with one word and release them. Pay attention to the new ones that come as they come. Think of it as lying in the grass and staring up at the sky. You see the clouds pass over. When the clouds go the sky is clear, just like your mind. Remember what the Eastern philosophy often states: you are not your mind, you are not your thoughts. You are not your emotions. You are not sad, you are not afraid, you are not excited nor depressed. These are just chemicals inside your brain and electrical impulses. You don't even have to continue your thoughts when they come. You are just a spectator of what's happening inside you. So observe and just let go. Emotions, feelings and thoughts come and go.

- Breathing

Pay attention to the shifts in your breathing patterns. They should slow as you focus on this moment. Be aware of the sensations of breathing. With breathing, there are two kinds: the kind where you take a deep breath and your chest expands and your shoulders will slightly rise and fall; alternatively, when you are breathing with your lower diaphragm, it is your belly that will rise and fall, while your chest does not expand at all. This deep "belly breathing" will literally lift the burden of even breathing off of your shoulders and will allow your physical awareness to go inward through breathing from your core.

Another thing that was the key for me to remember was that in all things, the focus needed to be me. I could not shift blame; I am a full-grown adult and I am responsible for myself. I certainly could not be overly critical of others. Picking other people apart gives the false impression of being a temporary fix for gaining self-confidence, but really it is confidence. This is your ego trying to sneak in and base your self-worth on the lack of perceived worth in others. If you compare, you will never be happy—ever.

Using your favorite heroes or inspirational people as encouragements and examples for personal growth are one thing; comparing yourself to those you perceive as "lesser" or "better" than you is a formula for death of your advancement in your personal self-improvement. When thinking negatively and tearing others down by comparing or judging them in my head, I was basically just wasting my energy, energy that I could have been investing in myself. This is time I could have been redirecting and investing into positively building myself up.

There will always be someone better or worse at something than you, and comparing will be a trap that is impossible to escape. Besides—what does it matter if someone is better or worse than you? Wouldn't you like to be confident and successful in your own right? When we are independently secure within ourselves, we open our minds to see the gifts that others can provide, without expectation but with extreme gratitude.

It dawned on me that my sole concentration needed to be on me. I needed to put all of my energy into myself. You will, too; others are a distraction. You have spent long enough, as I had, putting energy into others in order to boost your self-confidence. Decidedly, it is not always in a negative way, sometimes you just look to others to build your confidence in a positive way, which re-enforces your own value as a contributing member in society. Other times I just wanted to care for the people in my life. It is crucial that you must remember that you cannot take care of others when you yourself are broken.

I once purchased a simple little candle that had an affirmation written on it; the author of the affirmation is not known. However, during times of trial, this personally has helped every single person I have shared it with, and so I will also gift it to you, wishing you peace if you ever need to use it for yourself:

"This burden on my heart is too heavy to hold. I allow my spirit to grieve the loss of this dream. I allow my tears to cleanse me, freeing me from these crippling emotions. I release my expectations of the future and embrace the gifts this challenge has given me."

Now, do your best to commit these NLP tools to memory and get used to them. These are only few, but believe me, with meditation and anchoring alone you can change your personality entirely if you really stick to the process. Use all of the tools I gave you. Of course, everything takes time and consistency. Ironically, you will get much more consistent when your confidence level boosts up. This is the effect I call "the upward spiral": when you improve one thing, the rest gets better. There's also "the downward spiral" - when you neglect one aspect of your life, everything around it gets down and shrinks. And the former is exactly the effect you want to have in your life: the upward spiral, gaining more and more momentum everyday, building up positive emotions, actions and thoughts towards a successful life you want. And when you make it gain momentum and go really fast, at some level there's no way back. <u>No escape from success</u>.

Chapter 3 NLP During Your Self-Confidence Boost Journey

It is very important to stay focused when using NLP. Mindfulness is key. That is the most important information to take away from these lessons: staying focused and being aware and mindful is absolutely imperative. This point cannot be over-stressed.

A way to stay focused and keep focus is to concentrate on "NOW." What better way to stay in the now than to have a great morning routine? Starting every day with a routine centered on staying focused and reminding myself of the importance of that day makes all of the difference in the world. I could not think about yesterday, nor tomorrow. Focusing on the day at hand is a very important part of NLP.

In my beginning journey, every day was another opportunity for me to build my self-esteem. I had to take time to focus every single morning. It is way too easy to get distracted by other people and other priorities. Start off your day centering your mind around you and what you need to do.

DAILY AFFIRMATIONS AND GOALS (SHORT TERM)

It is important to start your day off right. It is also important to make sure you stay focused. An easy way to do this is through daily affirmations. Although these steps can initially appear to be time-consuming, you can accomplish them consciously in less than five minutes every single morning.

1. Find time to focus/meditate at the beginning of your day. find a quiet spot, even if it a common place in your residence.

2. Tell yourself five things that are positive about yourself. For every negative self-statement, it takes five positives simply to undo the harmful effect of one negative. Furthermore, I really recommend that you sit down for half an hour and write down a list of things you are proud of in your life. Make it as long as possible. It will make you feel better instantly and you will be extremely surprised of how much there is you don't remember and are not aware of everyday! You know what? Do it NOW. Take a piece of paper and write it down. Don't stop until your list has at least 35 positions on it. Mine has over 40. I wrote such things as, for instance: I have a nice, deep

voice, I can play guitar, I have travelled more than 20 countries, I'm a good cook, I go to gym regularly, I graduated good university in spite of many obstacles, I have nice facial hair, I know how to repair stuff, I've read many books, I can speak languages and so on... don't cheat, do it now! Promise yourself 35 positions or you don't eat your dinner and swap beds with your dog tonight. Read it every day. It's powerful. You'll see. Now let's go back to the morning routine:

3. Remind yourself of your high self-esteem and self-confidence. Repeat these words to yourself out-loud. There are many sites that will give different verbiage for positive affirmations, because not all wordings will work for everyone. However, for example, one powerful one that I used once was "I do not necessarily forgive right this moment, but I am open to the universe to forgive." Within two days, a former family member had approached me to apologize for his horrid behavior from two years earlier. So find a positive affirmation that speaks your language and gives you a sense of peace and reinforcement, even if it is as simply as "I am worthy of love and acceptance, I am confident in myself, I

value myself, and I deserve good things in life." You can also create your own affirmations. You should feel touched emotionally saying them out loud.

4. Tell yourself that you have control of yourself. You have the ability to do anything you want; be cautious to prevent negative thoughts from creeping in—until you are mentally able to do this part of the exercise, speaking out-loud to yourself or writing it down daily (again, really recommended) will be a good place to begin the habit until you are ready for the next step. Anytime you win over yourself and show strong will– write it down to a text file in your computer. I mean it.

5. While you are doing this, put yourself in the mindset of being tremendously confident with high self-esteem. Feel as if you have high self-confidence. Say out loud to yourself in the mirror, while looking into your own eyes, "I am worthy of all things that are lovely and good." Do it every morning and every evening.

Another simple yet effective way to stay focused every day is by setting simple goals for the day. The criteria for these goals should be:

1. They are realistic—over-whelming yourself with too much will only contribute to your sense of defeat if you fall short of your goal.

2. Ensure the goals will contribute to improving your situation in some way, shape or form.

3. Start small, and complete your tasks.

By setting goals every day, it will help you to be successful every day. This will inevitably help to boost your self-confidence. You will be realizing goals that you have set for yourself on a regular basis. Your self-esteem will get a boost every day from the tremendous sense of accomplishment!

A friend of mine was undergoing a difficult illness, and sometimes her goal was simply to gather the strength to go into the living room and socialize for a while with her mother. That was her daily success.

You know yourself better than anyone—do not put more on yourself than you can reasonably handle. In hard times, perhaps the goal is simply to get out of bed and get dressed and go to work. In good times, you might take a long hike and climb the nearest mountain. Either way, one of my primary pieces of advice in life is to listen to your body, and listen to it until you feel peace. This can translate to every form of your life! Set your goals, but also listen to your body and your mind and make the goals that bring you peace of mind within yourself. Be kind to yourself, and gentle. Refuse to allow anger or guilt to become a part of your being. It is poison and can only contagiously spread, defeating all of the NLP work that you are doing to change for the better.

A very wise woman, Eleanor Roosevelt, famously once said "No one can make you feel inferior without your consent." Truly dwell on the wisdom of that philosophical statement for a moment. You might be thinking, "Wait, what? People make me feel inferior all the time, and I sure as heck are not letting them do it—it just happens!" However, if you truthfully contemplate the thought, you will grow to learn it's powerful truth: you may receive negativity from others, but only you willingly give up the authority to allow them to make you feel influenced and inferior about yourself.

Now, granted, certainly no one wants to become so hardened that anything negative said towards you is something you dismiss as "I refuse to feel inferior!" or "I refuse to dwell on the negativity!" A crucial part of self-growth is being open to true, sincere constructive criticism. So if you receive a negative input from someone, think to yourself, "What can I learn from this? Is this a moment where I can draw a semblance of truth and find an area within myself to improve upon? Or was this something that I should dismiss because it was said in ignorance, pettiness, and is it damaging and no-conducive to self-growth?" Take the truth, even if it is negative, and turn it around into a positive. The benefits of this are two-fold: you are NOT allowing anyone to MAKE you feel inferior about yourself, and you are still allowing any opportunity to reveal you to yourself and to perhaps become aware of a shortcoming that you truly do want to improve upon. So you have cycled through the NLP behaviors by controlling your instinctive reactions and thoughts, which provide perspective on your emotions, which in turn translate to changing your actions.

I recently heard a blurb on the radio that "grateful people are more satisfied in life and report being generally happy than less-grateful people." It gave me an idea, and one that has actually truly contributed towards my daily outlook on life: I began my own personal "Thankfulness Jar." I cut lined 3x5 index cards in half, and every day I would date them and write something I was grateful for THAT DAY. A rule I gave myself was that it could not be too generic, such as "I am grateful for my health," or "I am grateful for the pretty sky." I had to find a specific thing from that exact day to search to be grateful for so I could put the card in my jar. And do you know what? I began to see things as moments to be grateful for, whereas prior to that those moments simply felt like everyday interactions of life.

For example, I remember near the end of the day while shopping in one of those buy-in-bulk warehouses, it was a crowded and busy day since a holiday was coming up shortly. I bought several smaller items and upon checkout, the nice lady asked me "Would you like a box for your things?" and I simply, pleasantly, and normally replied "Yes, please." She got a slightly surprised look on her face, which I did not really understand, then a moment later she said to the cashier and to myself, "Do you know what? I've been working an eight-hour shift all day, and do believe that you are the first 'yes, please' I have received all day!" I was aghast—this poor, sweet, hardworking girl was pleasantly serving me by doing her job at the very end of the retail day on a very busy shopping season, and yet somehow I was the first person to give a simple 'yes, please'? I made sure to re-affirm my appreciation for the compliment, to thank the staff again, and then I went on my way home. But I will tell you what—I had a wonderful encounter to write down for my gratefulness jar that day!

You seek out the moments to be grateful, and they will come to you. This consistency of actions will be a force within your life that begins to build bridges in places you did not even know existed.

Chapter 4 NLP to Maintain High Self-Confidence Forever and Never Feel Insecure Again

As anyone will testify, balance is essential in life. Too much of anything will cause a deficiency in another area of your life, and oftentimes that is simply not acceptable. One key to using NLP to maintain your confidence is to socialize and surround yourself with people who will support your new approach to life. One idea is to sit down and create a "life list" of simple things that you (1) currently enjoy doing, (2) have done in the past and would like to try again, and (3) new things you would love to learn or try. I created a bucket-list made of 80 goals. I've achieved some of them already, which makes me feel much better about myself and my life and gives me a lot of self-esteem. Find out what genuinely sparks your interest and then expand on that to build a new social life. For instance, if you love to read, join a book club. If you have always wanted to take a trip on a hot-air balloon, watch the internet for promotions and opportunities, even if you go by yourself. Doing things by yourself is nerve-wracking for everyone—even for those with confidence! However, although there are several benefits of socializing and going out more frequently, there is one part that most people overlook: if you go somewhere by yourself, you are basically forcing yourself to socialize with those around you, and you do not have your friend/partner/support person there to act as your "buffer" or "safety zone." If you go to a group hot-air balloon ride by yourself, hey, you are pretty much guaranteed to make new friends that have the same interests as you! Whether you are romantically single or not, it does not matter: doing activities and broadening your horizons within yourself is the key to instilling the permanent self-confidence that you have been working so hard to achieve.

I remember as a child, when I was in 5th grade, we all received awards for character qualities. I was such a dork that it is beyond description, but I was also very firm in my beliefs of right and wrong, and I was not afraid to stand up for them. I had just few friends, so it was surprising to me when I received the award for leadership. I will always remember what my teacher said when issuing the award; she said "Leadership does not always mean doing what is popular; leadership means doing what is right, even if no one else will follow." I am many decades beyond that moment, and yet when times are hard and I feel alone in my path choices to take the higher, happier, but more difficult road, I remember those words. We should all realize that we are our own leaders, choose within our best personal interests, and remember that it does not matter if anyone follows—because we have empowered ourselves and we are determined to never go back to that unhappy person we used to be.

This brings up another unfortunate but real part of life: most people have others in their lives that essentially will discourage, invalidate, and basically act as emotional leeches. Because these are often close personal relationships, such as long-time friends or family members, you will experience a sincere emotional conflict when choosing whether or not to continue exposing yourself to people who can bring you down and know how to push your emotional buttons. However, as has been repeatedly stated, the goal with this book is NOT to change others, but to reprogram our own thinking.

As a suggestion, while in the beginning stages of learning to reprogram yourself using the techniques of NLP, limit your interactions with these people in your life (if they must be in your life, that is). When you are stronger and more reinforced and in control of your cycle of thoughts, actions, emotions, and reactions, then you will be better prepared to face situations that have in the past proven detrimental to you. But life is a journey, and sometimes you need to walk off the beaten path for a while by yourself in order to arrive at the destination goal that you truly seek.

Remember how quality attracts quality? Well, the old proverbial phrase of "garbage in, garbage out" works the same way, too. Again, balance is the key. You cannot have a better social life if you feel poorly because you are not taking care of your basic, fundamental needs. Respect and take care of your body, take pride in your appearance, give your body the gift of good sleep, and stop wasting your time with superficial things such as constant television-watching and social media-checking. Sure, pick a few of your favorite things if you must, but 'garbage in, garbage out'—if you are filling your head with the latest drama of who is dating whom in Hollywood or what will happen on the next season of the latest evening 'soap opera-type' drama show, then that is time when you are NOT having fun doing something else! It might be basic and even contrite to say, but always go back to the basics: drink more water, exercise, eat better, sleep better, keep your head up (this alone makes you feel more confident), stimulate your mind with quality (read at least 10 pages of a good book everyday), surround yourself with warmth and light, and if you do not like something about yourself (such as low self-esteem) then work to change it! This is what you do if you want to get ahead: **COMPLETELY CUT OFF EVERYTHING THAT DOESN'T SUPPORT YOU.**

Start with the basics, retrain your brain using these effective and easy NLP techniques, and patiently watch, wait, and observe yourself slowly growing into the person you know you truly are and truly want to be! If you are in a job and have been eyeing a promotion, then start dressing more professionally and asking for more mentoring from those above you. Yes, I have to say it—sometimes you have to fake it until you make it! Did you know that smile (or even a fake smile) makes you feel better even if you are sad? It's a good example of anchoring- think about it. It's connected with good emotions in your brain. The same goes to other simple things, just as body language. Try to observe confident people, such as actors and rock stars, and then simply start to move and dress more like them (maybe you don't want to dress like glam rock 80's bands or look like some Hollywood psycho-stalker-mime-clone, but I guess you get the point – don't overdo it, but still it would be better than cringing with your head down and your arms curled). **DARE! You MAKE your life what you want it to be**, and in the process you will feel empowered to continue on with pursuing your path.

And let us not forget about that rut we can all so easily fall into in life! We do the same things, we see the same people, and we do not often allow ourselves to step outside our comfort zone! It is just easier that way, I understand, but it is also the best way to keep your life stagnant and boring. Make "go places and do things!" one of your new mottos! Yes, keep up with the routines of positive reinforcement discussed in this book, but also give yourself permission to try new and interesting things! Although it sounds contradictory, 'scheduling time for spontaneity and fun' is good for you! It will fill that need for balance that is so necessary to a happy, fulfilling life. Meditate daily, and utilize whatever means you have at your disposal to make the techniques work for you. Here are some ideas: keep a small daily notebook; draw a chart or diagram of your goals and break down the categories; paint or draw a picture; or even record yourself talking to yourself about your goals and dreams, kind of like verbal journaling. Different people have different learning methods, and you can find the one that best works for you. I keep my diary. Education, such as this book, should be approximately 20% of your journey, but the remaining 80% comes from ACTION. With this transformative process, you have a bright and exciting vision of what your life could really, truly be! Your dreams are within your grasp!

Remember, once you have started your journey towards change, the only thing that separates those who succeed and those who do not is perseverance and determination. DO NOT QUIT. Be patient, for it is a journey, but never, never give up.

You may fall, but you must stand back up every time, brush yourself off, and keep going—it is the only way to win! That and that alone, is how you find the real strength and confidence as a human being that we all so greatly deserve: by committing to a process and sticking to it!

Allow me to share a story: at my high school graduation, as tradition dictates, our principal (a seemingly grumpy, ex-military curmudgeonly old man) started out his address to the graduating seniors. Of course, he starts saying how he searched high and low through books from the greatest philosophers of our time for the best words of wisdom to share with us as we began our adult lives. Certainly, by this time I am rolling my eyes and am thinking, "Oh, this is going to be soooo boring." But then, he continues by saying "...and I found what I was looking for in the most unexpected of places: Winnie the Pooh's Little Book of Wisdom." I was at first shocked, then thrilled as he read us his favorite passages. Therefore, I will do the same. Using the unsurpassed wisdom of Winnie the Pooh, remember that just as Christopher Robin said to Pooh, "If ever there is tomorrow when we're not together, there is something you must always remember. You are braver than you believe, stronger than you seem, and smarter than you think." ~ A.A. Milne~

BONUS CHAPTER FROM IAN

The best lesson I got from life is: When they say you can't do it – just prove that you can F**** DO IT!!!**

I hope this bonus chapter will encourage you to stand up for yourself and your abilities. Here's an inescapable fact: Many people (possibly your friends or family!) feel insecure about themselves and want to make you feel the same way. They may be doing this on purpose; however, they may be doing it without bad intentions. They may be trying to protect you, in their own way. Some people are scared to see others succeed. It's deeply rooted in their mentality and meta-programs (the way they perceive the world - the subconscious controlling their thoughts and emotions).

In this chapter I share some of my own experiences based on WHAT OTHERS SAID and WHAT I DID. I hope it can inspire you.

I love travelling. I recognize it as a positive addiction - it can boost your self-confidence beyond imagination, especially when you arrange it on your own (without a travel agency) and go alone. After my senior year at the University I decided to finally take a Gap Year. Once I saw some beautiful picture galleries of Morocco on the Internet and had wanted to go there ever since. My sister lives in Spain, so I decided to fly to Barcelona and hitchhike down to Morocco from there – my first solo travel outside my continent.

Everyone said I couldn't do it. Spain is known as an extremely unfriendly place for hitchhikers. I don't know why, but almost every driver looks at you as you would look at a wet dog with a lame leg. The country is distinct among hitchhikers as meriting ten out of ten "difficulty stars" when it comes to catching a ride. My sister told me she'd seen many folks sitting on curbsides with their destination-cardboards, totally resigned after few days of waiting. I revealed my plans to my parents as well; they told me it was a stupid plan and I should go with a tourist agency (ha-ha!) because that's the "responsible way". My brother-in-law, a Spaniard who loves independent travelling as well and had been to Morocco before, told me I should take a bus because my travel plan was close to impossible. I spent a week in Barcelona and every time I shared my intentions with anyone, people just looked at me that disquieting way (like "calm down, boy, and just get yourself a plane there, or go home and play with your toy-cars"). I could listen to all those people – for sure they knew their own country better than me – but I simply didn't want to. I wanted to keep the promise I made to myself. A few days later I set out and… it was the hardest hitchhiking in my life indeed. I forgot to mention that at the time I didn't know any Spanish. Not a word. Maybe "gracias" and "por favor", but that was pretty much it. I had lots of adventures that first day and few times I came close to resigning, but I kept telling myself that I would do it and visualized myself inside a cool Moroccan truck or taking selfies in the Sahara – discarding dark thoughts and transforming them to positive energy. And I did it. I was stubborn enough in approaching and talking with people in each even though they couldn't speak English or said "no" (or worse) initially… and that's how I got myself a crazy ride all the way down to Morocco the very same day! I met lots of amazing people, saw extraordinary and beautiful places, spent almost two months in Africa and fulfilled one of my big dreams. Everyone told me I couldn't do it. I proved to myself I could. I'll never forget that.

***

Back in high school, there was this extraordinarily beautiful girl – slim, stylish, and intelligent as hell, who dressed well and moved with magical grace. She rejected all the guys who asked her out. I thought they must be doing something wrong and decided to do things my own way and take my chances. I found out the girl had interests I happened to share. I told my friends I want to asked her out and they almost killed me with laughter; they were sure there was no way a girl like that would date a pale, skinny boy like me. I wasn't sure either. She dated rarely, but only great-looking guys: basketball players, rich and popular dudes with jacked bodies, lead singers from local rock bands. Anyway, she always looked quite bored with them. After my research I decided to hit on her. Every time I approach a stranger girl I died of stress. I don't know why; she's a woman, probably weaker and slower than me, but somehow it's still overwhelming. Anyway, I just DO IT, knowing I'll just end up drowning in misery if I don't force myself. When I do, I always feel much better. I think of all my successes, strengths, hobbies and basically about how cool I was to hang out with. Even though I didn't look so good I wasn't the worst - I was using NLP without even knowing about it!

I sent her a message on the Internet, relating to one of her hobbies, and then, not waiting for an answer, approached her when she was sitting alone on a bench waiting for her lessons. It turned out she was really cool, a nice girl who liked me. First we took pictures (because she was keen on analog photography), but after five meetings we ended up in a relationship. I shut my friends up forever and had a great time.

Turned out she wasn't the love of my life but we stay good friends. I am happy I left my comfort zone and did things my own way. Now I'm sure I can meet and date a beautiful and smart girl. Otherwise I would have probably become another milksop coward guy who eventually turns into a hater of life and women.

Of course life is not all a bed of roses. Sometimes you stand up for something and the outcomes are different that you wished. I'm a slim guy and I catch colds too often. I've struggled with this problem as long as I can remember. I would start going to the gym and dieting, but every few months, despite a healthy diet, vitamins, etc., I get sick and have to stop. I also have stomach problems and it's hard to keep a balanced diet and eat as much as I should. After you stop it's hard to start again, since your body weakens even after a one month break. Regardless, I always return to the gym. Does it boost my self-confidence? You bet. I'm climbing up that mountain of success slowly, but I'm still going up and not surrendering to the obstacles!

Because you can never be defeated as long as you stand up from your knees, brush yourself off and keep climbing!

Conclusion – Your Personal Success for Life

Thank you again for downloading this book!

My greatest wish for you, my reader, is that you will take the messages and techniques in this book to feel an inner sense of peace and motivation to take action NOW!

As you have learned with these techniques, YOU are in control of your actions, your thoughts, and your choices! So the most important part in your life right now? GET STARTED NOW! Do one thing right now to advance your circumstances towards your goal. If necessary, start small, with saying an out-loud affirmation, such as "I will make changes. I am ready to be a more confident person. I am open-minded and welcome the change that is happening in my life from this moment forward." Or, if you are truly inspired to take a more significant step, then trust your instincts and do what you know you need to do! Listen to your body, and pay attention to the inner voice that tells you that you truly do know what you want and you know how to get it.

You will, without fail, see the effects of your choices immediately! More importantly, you will feel the effects—you will even have a slightly different outlook on the rest of your current day. Things are awakened, and you are ready!

We all know: life is difficult, and can often be painful—but by taking ACTION, you join an exclusive club of people who choose to do the hardest thing of all: self-empowerment for self-improvement! And do you know why you have chosen to be part of the estimated 1% of people who choose to face this challenge? It is because deep down inside of you, you KNOW beyond a shadow of a doubt that you are better than the low self-esteem demons that have been plaguing you for so long. You not only want more out of life, but you DEMAND more out of life! Make a pledge to yourself to do one thing immediately to take action as a symbol to yourself that you have begun your new life's journey for happiness, self-esteem, self-confidence, and a permanent escape from your former, unhappier self—because, truly, you have already grown beyond that unhappy person! You are reading this book! You are motivated to make changes, because they simple yet significant changes, and you know you can do them!
You are fighting this fight, accepting this challenge, and taking on this adventure because you seek a better tomorrow and a fulfilling life.

Finally, if you enjoyed this book, please – take a few minutes of your time to share your thoughts and post

a review on Amazon (http://www.amazon.com/dp/B00IEJSJ0C). It would be greatly appreciated as your feedback will encourage me to create more books for you to enjoy!

Thank You again for your interest in my work,
Ian

Recommended Reading for You:

If you are interested in Self-Development, NLP, Psychology, Social Dynamics, Soft Skills and related topics, you might be interested in previewing or downloading the following:

My book: <u>Improve Your Relationship Fast with NLP</u>
http://www.amazon.com/dp/B00J70HWYG/

All interpersonal conflicts have three key ingredients; **wrong perceptions, improper communication and destructive behavioral patterns.**
NLP gives us simple and yet effective techniques to **redirect those perceptions, significantly enhance communication** with the people we care about and **reprogram those negative behavioral patterns** forever so that our relationships can flourish! In this book not only I'll show you the **most effective NLP tools in the context of permanent relationship improvement**, but also my mindset, the right approach that actually works in relationships and I'll tell you **how to enhance**

your communication skills and how to start a journey towards being a better partner and family member!

My book: Stress Management With NLP
http://www.amazon.com/dp/B00JGVZ8L0/

I was always stressed to the max. When I was young, **I was called a worry-wart and told that I would have a heart-attack, ulcer or be bald by the age of 16.**
At some point of my life I came to the conclusion that my nervousness got way too dangerous and **I HAD** to find a solution and **finally calm down**. I would read books, watch DVD's, talk to people and go to seminars. And then – finally - I found the answer. **In this book I'll show you NLP tools tailor-made for stress and anxiety management** and my favorite **relaxation techniques that helped me.** You will also read how to **minimize stressors and adverse circumstances** that keep you **anxious and nervous** and about the **right mindset and lifestyle you should have to maintain low stress level, finally relax and stop worrying...**

My Mailing list: If you would like to receive fresh info about **new Kindle reads** on social dynamics, psychology, career, NLP, success and healthy living for **free** (or deeply **discounted – as low as $0,99**) I invite you to my Mailing List. Whenever my new book is out, I set the promotional price/free period for two days. You will get an e-mail notification and will **be the first to get the book for $0,99 (or free)** during its limited promotion.

Why would I do this when it took me countless hours to write these e-books?

First of all, that's my way of saying **"thank you"** to my new readers. Second of all – **I want to spread the word about my books and ideas.** Mind you that **I hate spam and e-mails that come too frequently** - no worries about that.
If you think that's a good idea and are in, just surf there: http://eepurl.com/R_UhP

Also, follow me on Twitter: https://twitter.com/IanTuhovsky

Simply follow us on Facebook:

www.facebook.com/HolisticWellnessBooks

We have created this page with a few fellow authors of mine. We hope you find it inspiring and helpful.

Thank You for your time and interest in our work!

Ian & Holistic Wellness eBooks

About The Author

Ian is an avid reader and writer and he calls himself "the observer of people and reality". He had always been interested in studying the human mind and the society. Ian holds a BA degree in Sociology and apart from writing and investigation he works as a HR consultant for many European companies from various sectors.

In his free time he really enjoys travelling and getting to know different cultures. His favorite way of travelling is a spontaneous, adventurous travelling on a very little budget- something he has been doing since he was a teenager and became a part of his lifestyle. Hitchhiking, as well as using services like "couch surfing" are his preferred modes of immersing himself into new cultures and staying out of his comfort zone. He just loves the thrill of unpredictable travelling!

Another passion of Ian's is music. He plays the guitar, sings and composes music. He is also an electronic music producer- something he does as a hobby.

As a child and a teenager, Ian suffered from shyness and low self-esteem. Looking for solutions he would find consolation in doing lots of reading and writing songs. It wasn't until he began to confront his fears and do exactly the opposite that his brain was telling him. He likes putting his experiences on paper, who knows maybe they can inspire you in a way?

Printed in Great Britain
by Amazon